Contents

Part 1: Getting Started   1

Why choose the low-carb lifestyle?.................2

What is low-carb?...3

The history of low-carb living..........................4

Why low-carb diets work.....................................6

When you start a low-carb diet..................... 10

Which low-carb diet is right for you?.......... 13

The Atkins Nutritional Approach................. 14

Protein Power... 15

The Zone... 16

Sugar Busters!... 17

Neanderthin.. 18

Somersizing... 19

The Schwarzbein Principle 20

The Carbohydrate Addict's Diet................... 21

GO-Diet.. 22

Life Without Bread.. 23

Your Fat Can Make You Thin 24

The Insulin Resistance Diet 25

The South Beach Diet... 26

Beyond Atkins... 27

The Hamptons Diet.. 28

Part 2: Low-carb Myths Debunked   29

Myth: Ketosis is dangerous............................. 30

Myth: You must measure for ketones......... 31

Myth: A calorie is a calorie is a calorie 32

Myth: Low-carb eating is not balanced..... 33

Myth: Low-carb eating will raise your

   cholesterol.. 34

**Part 3: Eight Things You Should Do—
and Two You Shouldn't—on Any
Low-Carb Diet**   35

DO: Drink lots of water 36

DO: Exercise! 37

DO: Take good-quality supplements

   regularly.. 38

DO: Keep a food diary.. 39

DO: Be a smart medical consumer.............. 41

DO: Find some kind of outside support 42

DO: Resist negative pressure from family

   or friends.. 43

DO: Follow your plan religiously.................. 44

DO NOT: Put too much emphasis on your

   scale weight... 45

DO NOT: Eat a bunch of low-carb

   "junk".. 46

**Part 4: Suggestions for Shopping and
Preparing Meals**   47

Plan and prepare to succeed.......................... 48

Shop first 49

Prepare some food for later............................ 51

Now, enjoy!... 53

Part 5: Additional Resources   55

Recommended reading....................................... 56

Online resources 57

About the author.. 60

"Yeah, I'd pay five bucks to learn more about that...."

- *Learn the iPod for 5 Bucks* ISBN 0321287851
- *Learn How to Buy and Sell on eBay for 5 Bucks* ISBN 0321287843
- *Learn the Canon EOS Digital Rebel Camera for 5 Bucks* ISBN 0321287827
- *Learn the Nikon Coolpix Camera for 5 Bucks* ISBN 0321287835
- *Learn How to Make Great Digital Photos for 5 Bucks* ISBN 032130361X
- *Learn the Low-Carb Lifestyle for 5 Bucks* ISBN 0321303601
- *Learn How to Win at Texas Hold 'Em Poker for 5 Bucks* ISBN 0321287819

Look for these terrific little books in all kinds of stores, everywhere. Lots more neat little "books for people who hate reading the manual" are on the way.

Keep checking **www.fairshakepress.com**. We'd love to hear what you'd pay five bucks to learn more about...

FairShake
press

Learn the Low-Carb Lifestyle for 5 Bucks

Karen Rysavy

Fair Shake Press, an imprint of Pearson Technology Group, division of Pearson Education

Composed in the typeface Cronos MM from Adobe Systems

ISBN 0-321-30360-1

9 8 7 6 5 4 3 2 1

Printed and bound in the United States of America

How to use this book

This book is a thorough yet concise introduction to low-carbohydrate diets. It won't teach you *everything* you need to know about low-carb diet plans, but it will get you off to a great start.

This book is not a substitute for a doctor-designed plan, but it is an invaluable resource to anyone interested in learning the basics of a low-carb lifestyle without breaking the bank. The author writes from experience—she lost ten dress sizes in under a year and lowered her cholesterol hundreds of points.

You can use this book to become healthier, slimmer, and more energetic, too!

- Learn the basics of all the most popular low-carb plans.
- Understand the science—presented in everyday terms that *anyone* can follow.
- Get the real low-down on the myths associated with low-carb diets.

Including all the important tips, pointers, and dos and don'ts that will help you make the most of whichever low-carb plan you ultimately decide to follow, this book is the mandatory first stop for anyone who is considering heading down the low-carb road.

Part 1

Getting Started

> *My story*

M y name is Karen, and, yes, that's really me in that awful "before" picture. But because I now live (and love!) a low-carb lifestyle, I'm confident that I will never look like that again. Nor must I endure endless lectures when I see the doctor, because a low-carb lifestyle normalized my cholesterol as well as my weight. In fact, there is little about my health that didn't improve, once I changed my eating habits.

before low-carb   *after 1 year*

In early 2000, at age 34, I weighed 271 pounds and my cholesterol levels were off the charts. I'd become tired of fighting a losing battle with my weight years before, and had pretty much given up. Each time I had tried to lose weight by traditional means (restricting fat and calories), I would lose some weight, but then the loss would slow until it stopped altogether, despite continued adherence to the diet. I never felt well while dieting, and I was always starving. It is easy to see why I would become discouraged and quit, time after time. I now know that those early attempts to lose weight backfired not because I was doing anything wrong or not following the plans properly, but because the diets were further slowing an already sluggish metabolism, dooming me to gain back more than I lost, every time.

When my husband announced that he was going to "start that Atkins thing," the first words out of my mouth were, "Oh no, you're not! Those low-carb diets are dangerous!" "How do you know?" he challenged me. I had to admit then that I didn't know enough about them to have a truly informed opinion, and I decided to look into low-carb diets with an open mind.

I began by reading every book I could find on the subject. By the time I got to the second chapter of the first book I read, I was smiling and nodding along. These plans made a lot of sense and they could be applied in a healthy and balanced manner. The promise of weight loss without hunger sealed the deal, and I decided to try a low-carb diet along with my husband. For the first time in years, I had hope.

That hope did not disappoint. All those wild promises of better health, more energy, and almost effortless weight loss and maintenance held true. You, too, can find low-carb success! This book will introduce you to basic principles and put you on the path to success by helping you choose the plan that is right for you.

"L ow-carbing" is not new—this way of eating has been around literally since the time of cave dwellers. In fact, some of the strictest low-carb diets make a conscious effort to emulate our prehistoric diet as closely as possible.

Archaeology shows us unmistakably that humans are far healthier as a species when we live a "hunter-gatherer" lifestyle than when we settle down to a more agricultural and less protein-based existence. Human remains from newly agricultural-based societies are much smaller in stature than the remains of their hunter-gatherer ancestors. In addition, these urban farmers had a significantly shorter average life span than their ancestors, while displaying many signs of poor health previously unfound in those societies.

Ancient Egypt is an excellent example. While this trend has been repeated in many other societies through history, the Egyptian mummies provide an abundance of proof of the decline in health caused by excess consumption of refined carbohydrates and low protein consumption. The mummies tell us that many ancient Egyptians were obese, suffering from disorders like advanced heart disease, cancerous tumors, and even diabetes. Clearly, the biggest difference in their lives before and after this sharp decline in their health was diet-based. The Egyptians established their advanced society largely because of new technology that allowed them to grow, store, and disperse large quantities of grain, ending periodic famines and facilitating the movement of their armies. Their new diet based on grain-based foods came at a high price biologically, however.

Societies that have remained healthy throughout history while subsisting on a primitive diet of meat, fish, seeds, nuts, and native vegetables and fruits show the greatest increase in diabetes and other "disorders of civilization" when suddenly exposed to a modern diet based primarily on refined carbohydrates. It appears that the longer a society has subsisted on a "modern" diet, the better it tolerates that diet as a group … but at this rate, it will take many thousands more years before we can make a real evolutionary switch.

Fortunately, we don't have to continue to suffer through the pangs of evolution. All we have to do is go back to the way we were meant to eat, which just happens to be the low-carb way.

William Banting. Modern low-carb diets got their real start back in the Victorian era. Although there were other proponents from earlier times, it was a middle-aged Englishman named William Banting who really popularized the diet in the 1860's when he published and distributed 2500 copies (at his own expense) of the first known diet plan written in English. Titled *Letter on Corpulence*, this is undoubtedly the grandfather of all modern low-carb diets.

Banting didn't attempt to explain why his eating plan worked. He just knew that following the advice of his doctor by restricting sweet and starchy foods, while still eating all he wanted of other foods, worked well and didn't leave him hungry. Banting went from being so obese that he had to go down stairs backward to avoid falling over to being a man of normal stature. He had actually been going deaf from the pressure of excess fat on his ear drums, before he adopted a low-carb eating plan. (Now, that's fat!) He stuck to "Banting," as his diet plan came to be popularly called, for the rest of life and lived to a quite respectable (especially for those days) age of 81.

Vilhjalmur Stefansson. The next big round of publicity for low-carb came in the 1920s, when a Swede named Vilhjalmur Stefansson became intrigued with the Eskimo practice of subsisting on nothing but meat and fat for months at a time. He decided to conduct an experiment to see if a "civilized" man could thrive on the same diet. For an entire year, while under close observation at Bellevue Hospital in New York, he had nothing but fresh meat and water. Contrary to the expectations of many, he emerged after the yearlong experiment seemingly healthy, several pounds lighter, and with lower serum cholesterol than when he started.

Weston A. Price. In the 1930s, Weston A. Price, a Cleveland dentist, became disturbed about the rampant decay and crowded teeth he was observing in his patients, accompanied by what he termed worsening facial deformities. He theorized that the new foods that had become available after the Industrial Revolution were responsible for the change, and he spent the next ten years visiting primitive peoples around the world and documenting the dramatic physical changes and sudden disease that accompanied the introduction of refined foods in place of traditional ones. His photographic evidence is quite dramatic and has remained in print from 1939 to the present, in a book titled *Nutrition and Physical Degeneration*.

Robert Atkins. Finally, in the latter half of the 20th century, several doctors publicly embraced various forms of low-carb dieting, including Herman Tarnower, Irwin Stillman, and Alfred Pennington. But it was Robert Atkins and then Michael and Mary Dan Eades who really took up the cause of low-carb eating, refusing to quietly accept traditional dogma on nutrition and in the process forever changing the world's ideas about the role of food in relation to good health.

When studies proving that a low-carb diet was both safe and effective in at least the short term were published in several prestigious medical journals and then consistently repeated, the medical establishment was forced to sit up and take notice. Atkins particularly had to endure decades of public ridicule before finally getting some of the credit he so richly deserved just before his accidental death due to complications of a fall in April 2003.

Michael and Mary Dan Eades. Michael and Mary Dan Eades, the aforementioned husband-and-wife team of practicing doctors and co-authors of the Protein Power books, are the original inventors of the Deduct Dietary Fiber rule, which Atkins and others later adopted. The Eades's theories were and are ground-breaking, and the Eadeses deserve as much credit for the recent vindication of low-carb diets as does Atkins.

And the rest. More recently, a slew of other experts have published their own variations on the low-carb diet, not least among them the instantly popular South Beach Diet and the even more moderate Zone Diet. All of the best-known low-carb plans have something to recommend them, and I will highlight the basic principles of each later on in this book, to try to help you choose the plan that is most likely to work for you.

TIP:

This is my definition of low-carb: Eat simply. Eat lots of fresh food, real food, that you prepare yourself—no food out of a box, no grains (at least at first), and no food that has been chemically altered (no junk!) Eat meat, fish, vegetables, nuts and seeds, fruit, and dairy products—and eat them pretty much in that order.

The basic underlying principles of low-carb diets fly in the face of decades of entrenched medical recommendations—recommendations that are increasingly regarded as more theory than fact by the nutritionists, researchers, and physicians who make up the medical establishment.

Our current food pyramid was based on nothing more than a theory that the fat and cholesterol we eat are what most affect our eventual body fat and serum cholesterol. Sounded reasonable at the time, but in practice this supposition has failed miserably. The real culprit responsible for most cases of elevated cholesterol, heart disease and obesity is actually insulin resistance, which is sometimes referred to as hyperinsulinemia, syndrome X, or metabolic syndrome.

Insulin resistance is a normal effect of aging, but it can be brought on early (and severely) by excess consumption of refined carbohydrates over a long period of time. This is fairly easy to see, in hindsight. Just stop to consider the fact that we in America have grown steadily fatter and fatter over the last 30 years, despite eating steadily decreasing amounts of dietary fat and protein all that time. Why did the recommended low-fat diet fail so miserably, for most people?

There are three main classes of foods:
• Proteins
• Fats
• Carbohydrates

Only two of these components are truly essential to human life: protein and fat. Your body is more than capable of manufacturing its own carbohydrates for energy, and will do so quite efficiently when called to the task.

Not so with fat and protein. Out of about 20 identified amino acids, there are 8 essential amino acids found in protein that our body cannot manufacture by itself, and they must therefore be provided in our diet.

TIP: *Vegetarians should note that the only single food source on earth that contains all eight of the essential amino acids is meat. You can low-carb as a vegetarian, but it will be more difficult to do so healthfully.*

> *The science in everyday terms*

Fat contains two known acids (linolenic acid and alpha-linolenic acid) that are similarly essential to life and must also be provided in the food we eat. Both of these essential fatty acids are found in meat, as well as fish, various nuts and seeds, and vegetable oils.

Carbohydrates are broken down into two classes—simple and complex—but all you need to remember is this: All carbohydrates are forms of sugar. The only real difference on a cellular level between a simple carbohydrate and a complex carbohydrate is the speed at which they are absorbed during digestion and subsequently turned into glucose.

Glucose is the fuel that provides energy to feed and maintain all our cells. When there is a steady supply of carbohydrates present in the diet, the body takes what it needs for its immediate energy requirements and stores any excess in the form of body fat, where it will remain accessible for later use. This is a wonderful survival trait for humans as a species, and it comes in handy during times of famine—but in times of plenty, it condemns individuals to store more and more body fat over time. Only the prospect of imminent starvation can induce the body to access and reduce its fat store, and once the body realizes that its precious store is dwindling, it automatically slows down its metabolic rate in order to make the remaining stored fat last as long as possible. This is why a low-fat diet can work well in the short term but proves so difficult to sustain over time. Our bodies are actively working against us at all times to build up (or preserve) a surplus of stored fat.

To mitigate this tendency of our bodies to want to be fat, we need to access the fat stores by turning on fat-burning. Traditional dieting theory tells us that the only way to do that is to burn more calories than you eat, but the low-carb approach emphasizes instead that the best and fastest way to access the fat store is to steeply limit the intake of carbohydrates while not limiting overall calories to the point that the body's "famine alarm" goes off to slow down or stop the process.

When the body is forced to resort to its stored fat reserves (also known as *adipose tissue*) to supply its immediate carbohydrate energy needs, it may have to work a little harder than it does when it uses freshly ingested carbohydrates for energy. Some have theorized that this extra process is responsible for the documented phenomenon that enables low-carb dieters to lose more weight while eating more calories than low-fat dieters.

"If it is that simple, then what's all this I keep hearing about insulin?" you ask. I am getting to that.

Not much about the way our bodies work is really simple. In fact, there are millions of different metabolic processes occurring in our bodies at all times. Each process works as a part of the whole, and if even one of those systems gets out of balance, the whole body can be adversely affected. (Think of the domino effect.)

One of the most complex mechanisms in our bodies regulates hormones. Hormones are ultimately responsible for all the major life processes—they control when and how we grow, at what rate we age, and even when one part of the body should attack another part for the good of the whole (the immune system). In the case of white blood cells fighting infection, this self-attack plan has a lot of merit, but other times the body attacks itself for largely unknown reasons. When this happens, we call the resulting problems *autoimmune disorders*. Autoimmune disorders include such ailments as arthritis, multiple sclerosis, polycystic ovary syndrome (PCOS), fibromyalgia, lupus, Crohn's disease, and diabetes, to name just a few.

Of all the known hormones, insulin is perhaps the most powerful and far-reaching. Insulin is created in the pancreas and used by the body to precisely regulate at all times the total amount of glucose in our blood (the *blood sugar level*), as well as to facilitate the storage of excess glucose. You can think of insulin as the fat-storage hormone. Glucose in the bloodstream is first conveyed by insulin to the muscles, where it is stored for short-term use as glycogen. Once the muscles have their fill of glycogen, any remaining excess glucose is converted by insulin into adipose tissue (fat!)

In very simplistic terms, when things are working normally, it goes like this: You eat something, and digestion begins. Glucose is created fairly rapidly from the carbohydrate content in the food, and as the newly created glucose is released into the bloodstream, a corresponding amount of insulin is secreted by the pancreas, to deal with the glucose and move it where it needs to go, keeping things in ideal balance.

> *The science in everyday terms*

A few people can seemingly eat all the carbohydrates in the world, and this system will continue to work well for them indefinitely. Others (the majority of people) are not so lucky.

While it is normal for our bodies to develop some resistance to the effects of insulin over the course of a lifetime, years of excess carbohydrate consumption can cause the insulin receptors in our cells to wear out early. The pancreas must then produce increasingly larger amounts of insulin in order to achieve the same affect. When the insulin receptors cease to function or the pancreas fails from continued overuse, full-blown diabetes results.

In the shorter term, the presence of excess insulin can cause other serious problems, including an increase in both triglycerides and water retention, thickening of the arterial walls (leading to high blood pressure), an increase in the reproduction rate of cancerous cells, and, perhaps most pertinent to this discussion, continued weight gain even when total calories consumed are not excessive.

The good news is, insulin receptors can be healed (and metabolism normalized) simply by restricting the intake of carbohydrates. You must remember, no matter how many times you have heard just the opposite, that an exceptionally strong argument is being made—and increasingly accepted in the medical establishment—that carbohydrates are not essential to good health. Carbohydrate restriction can help you lose weight without hunger, while balancing hormone levels in the body (and that can lead to a myriad of additional health benefits). Low-carb diets are well known for their ability to eliminate or at least reduce the severity of mood swings, acid reflux (heartburn), and many other gastrointestinal disorders, while improving energy levels and strengthening the immune system. Low-carb eating may even improve the odds of fertility—so good luck, or be careful, whichever the case may be!

When you start a low-carb diet

> *What to expect*

Several things can be expected when you shut down your body's carbohydrate supply suddenly (a required part of some low-carb diets, but not included in all of them):

Energy slump. Within 48 to 72 hours, the supply of glycogen in your muscles will run out, and you are likely to experience a huge energy slump, perhaps even flulike symptoms. This can be accompanied by a fierce headache and feelings of nausea. Don't give up—these are all good signs, believe it or not. These temporary symptoms are signs that your body is preparing to change the way it procures its energy—in other words, you are about to successfully access and then begin to transform your fat stores into usable energy by entering into a state of benign dietary ketosis, referred to after this as just *ketosis*.

Change in body fluid levels. Your kidneys will receive a signal telling them to release excess sodium and fluid from your now-glycogen-depleted muscles, and you will start to shed "water weight" rapidly. (Plan to visit the bathroom a lot for a couple of days!) This sudden change in body fluid levels can also cause an imbalance in your potassium level, and this imbalance *might* manifest itself as light-headedness or fatigue accompanied by changes in blood pressure and/or pulse rate.

You can prevent the effects of a sudden change in body fluid levels in almost all cases just by taking an inexpensive potassium supplement from the start. I strongly recommend a supplement of a least 100–200 mg of elemental potassium per day, along with a complete multivitamin, for all healthy people who are beginning a low-carb diet and do not have a medical condition that prohibits potassium supplementation. Potassium can provide relief from the worst of these symptoms, in most cases, within 20 minutes of taking it. Dosage can be increased up to 400 mg per day, if needed. Do yourself a favor—take the potassium from the beginning.

Warning: Certain blood pressure and other medications can cause a bad reaction when taken·in combination with potassium. If you are currently taking medications of any kind or have any specific health problems, you should consult your personal physician before beginning this (or any new) supplement regimen or diet of any kind.

TIP: *The front of the potassium supplement bottle may say something like 550 mg, but the back label, where the important data is, should list elemental potassium. That's the dose that counts!*

> *What to expect*

You may experience a distinct lack of appetite after the first few days, even temporary nausea. You must ensure that you are eating an adequate amount of fat and protein during this time, however, in order to provide your body with all the tools it needs to successfully convert itself over to a fat-based (ketogenic) energy system.

You may also find yourself feeling extremely hungry at other times. When that happens, be sure to eat!

Most low-carb diets are much more about *what* you eat and not about *how much*, especially at the beginning. Be sure to select foods containing mostly fat and protein, which are your primary energy sources and which will therefore be the most satisfying. Consult individual plans for guidance on which fats you should be eating, but you can pretty much throw everything you ever heard about restricting fat and calories in the past out the window. At this point in a low-carb plan, fat is most definitely your friend. Failing to eat regularly, and failing to include sufficient fat and protein content when you do eat, not only will *not* make you lose weight any faster, it can be counter-productive. Think of your metabolism as a furnace that you need to keep burning evenly. If you wait too long to feed the fire (eat) and let the flame go all the way out, then it will take a long time to for it get "hot" again. Many plan authors advise never going more than four waking hours without eating a little something—the trick is choosing the "something" wisely.

Once your body has successfully adjusted to burning fat for energy instead of carbs, which should occur within seven to ten days, your blood sugar levels will stabilize (perhaps for the first time ever!), and you can expect to enjoy a huge rush of energy accompanied by a feeling of overall well-being that leads many low-carb dieters to proclaim themselves "low-carb for life" on the spot.

If you follow one of the more moderate low-carb diet plans, you might not experience the most dramatic "down" symptoms detailed here—but you may also never experience the dramatic energy rush I mentioned, which I believe comes hand-in-hand with a state of full ketosis. Ketosis is not necessary for low-carb success, however. You can still achieve all the same wonderful weight loss and health benefits, no matter which low-carb plan you ultimately adopt, as long as you are willing to make the necessary lifelong (not just temporary) changes.

Now, don't panic! "Making lifelong changes" does *not* mean that you will never enjoy a carb again, I promise. It does mean that until you reach maintenance and have allowed your insulin receptors sufficient time to heal, you will have to be very careful in each and every one of your carb choices. You will be able to successfully incorporate more and more "good carbs," the longer you follow a low-carb lifestyle, but you will never be able to (nor will you want to!) return to your old ways and go back to eating lots of refined "bad carbohydrates."

One of my favorite definitions of insanity is "doing the same thing over and over and expecting a different result." A lot of people do this where diets are concerned. They seem to think they can make some changes for a while, lose the weight, and then "go off the diet" and somehow maintain the loss. It doesn't work that way. *Don't kid yourself.*

Fortunately, I find the prospect of eating this way for the rest of my life delightful! I eat much more food now than I ever did when I was obese, and I enjoy every morsel, because I find low-carb eating infinitely more versatile (see page 53) and satisfying than low-fat. Try it for a couple of weeks, and see for yourself. C'mon ... you know darned well that you can do *anything* for just two weeks! You should be able to tell, that fast, whether low-carb is right for you. You have nothing to lose by trying (besides excess weight and poor health).

Which low-carb diet is right for you?

Almost any low-carb plan can work successfully, but having a specific plan to follow and to refer back to, especially at the beginning, is crucial. Many of us who low-carb for a long time eventually customize the plan we follow, and that's appropriate. As individuals, we react differently to things, and we should make accommodations for those differences. But before you do that, you need to have a solid understanding of the physiological processes involved in low-carbing.

At the same time, there are some basic dos and don'ts to living a low-carb lifestyle that apply to every low-carb diet plan. This book won't really teach you how to low-carb; it's not a substitute for a doctor-designed plan. Instead, it is both an introduction to low-carb principles and a tool to help you choose and then get the most out of the low-carb plan you ultimately adopt.

I've included summaries of the best-known low-carb diets, as well as some that you may never have heard of:

- *The Atkins Nutritional Approach*
- *Protein Power*
- *The Zone*
- *Sugar Busters!*
- *Neanderthin*
- *Somersizing*
- *The Schwarzbein Principle*
- *The Carbohydrate Addict's Diet*
- *GO-Diet*
- *Life Without Bread*
  Your Fat Can Make You Thin
- *The Insulin-Resistance Diet*
- *The South Beach Diet*
- *Beyond Atkins*
- *The Hamptons Diet*

Most of these plans include specific recommendations regarding exercise and stress and emotional management. Because we all know that addressing those things should be a part of your life no matter *how* you eat, this book concentrates exclusively on the dietary aspects of the plans.

The recent interest in low-carb diets is the inevitable result of their success and popularity. There are obviously a lot more plans out there than I can discuss in the scope of this book. I limited my summary to the plans listed because I believe that they provide a good cross-section of the various theories. This should not be interpreted as an endorsement for any specific low-carb plan. Only you (with the advice of your physician) can make this decision—but I'll help you by telling you a little about each of the plans mentioned. Then you should investigate more thoroughly the plan(s) that interest you.

The Atkins Nutritional Approach

> Robert C. Atkins, M.D.

Originally published way back in the 1970s as *Dr. Atkins' Diet Revolution*, the Atkins plan has been refined and republished several times since, both as *Dr. Atkins' New Diet Revolution* and most recently as *Atkins for Life*. Atkins relies on your ability to reach a state of ketosis and stay there until your weight goal is reached. All of the books include specific food lists and lots of recipes to get you started.

The initial phase of Atkins, known as Induction, lasts for just two weeks and limits you to 20 net carbs per day. *Net carbs* are defined as total carbohydrates minus fiber and other ingredients thought not to directly affect blood sugar levels, including sugar alcohols (a form of artificial sweetener) and glycerin. Induction meals consist mostly of unprocessed meats, fish, and eggs, with good fats like olive oil, a limited amount of dairy products, and plenty of low-carb, high-fiber vegetables.

After the induction period, dieters increase their daily carbs by five per day, for a week at a time—in other words, during week three you would eat 25 carbs each day; during week four, 30 carbs per day; and so on. Dieters continue to increase carbs in this way until they stop losing weight. At that point, they drop back down to the previous level and stay there. The final phase, Lifetime Maintenance, is an eating plan designed to keep you healthy and fit for life, while allowing as many good carbs as you can personally tolerate.

While the Atkins plan has not always encouraged the regular consumption of vegetables, fruit, and even whole grains, the most recent versions of the plan do indeed encourage you to eat these foods. While you can eat foods like red meat, cream, and cheese as part of the plan, over-consumption of these foods is discouraged. Atkins has been most criticized for not unduly restricting saturated fat, but to date the consumption of saturated fat has not been proved to be harmful in the absence of excessive carbohydrates, while the diet has proved successful for millions.

The Atkins Nutritional Approach
- Encourages ketosis.
- Complete ban on refined carbohydrates, strict limits on other carbohydrates.
- Increases carbohydrates over time.
- Alcohol allowed in moderation after the first two weeks, with red wine or pure spirits preferred.

Protein Power

> *Michael R. Eades, M.D., and Mary Dan Eades, M.D.*

This plan is covered in *Protein Power, The Protein Power Lifeplan*, and *The 30-Day Low-Carb Diet Solution*, all recommended reading for anyone interested in the healing and preventative properties of low-carb nutrition as it relates to good overall health.

The Eades plan thoroughly explains which foods contain what they consider to be "good" versus "bad" fats, and stress the importance of dietary fiber intake while balancing the types of fat we eat. They believe imbalances of omega fatty acids in modern-day diets are ultimately responsible for many health problems in addition to weight gain, and they give clear instructions in their diet as to how to correct this imbalance. They are quite specific in their protein recommendations and are often thought of as "high-protein" advocates, but most low-carb advocates consider their plan merely "adequate-protein."

Ketosis is not encouraged as necessary, nor condemned as undesirable. The emphasis is on the quality of the foods you eat, while adhering to the carb restrictions and the protein guidelines.

The Protein Power plan includes valuable information for vegetarians who want to reap the benefits of low-carb eating, and addresses all aspects of health in some way, including exercise, supplements, sun therapy, and even calisthenics for the brain. The books comprising this plan are packed with specific food lists, menus, and recipes that make following this plan easy.

The Eadeses present compelling evidence to back up assertions that total cholesterol numbers are not as important as the makeup of the actual cholesterol particles present, and they discourage the use of cholesterol-lowering statin drugs. They feel that current cholesterol guidelines are far lower than is necessary for optimum health and back this opinion up with a wealth of medical data. I consider this plan a must-read for anyone battling elevated cholesterol, as well as anyone suffering from any type of autoimmune disease.

Protein Power
- Adequate protein intake stressed.
- Good fats encouraged over bad ones.
- Plenty of fruits and vegetables allowed during all phases.
- Adequate fiber intake stressed; this plan invented the "deduct dietary fiber" rule.
- Alcohol allowed in moderation, with red wine preferred.

The Zone

> *Barry Sears, Ph.D.*

Published in 1995, *The Zone* stands apart from most other low-carb plans because it is intended to be a moderate-carb, moderate-protein, and moderate-fat diet. The Zone does restrict carbohydrates greatly in comparison with the current USDA diet recommendations, however, leading most people to classify it as a low-carb diet.

Author Barry Sears encourages dieters to "enter the Zone" by ensuring that 40 percent of all calories ingested come from "favorable" carbohydrates, 40 percent from good fats, and 30 percent from low-fat protein. The plan places a very strict limit on saturated fat, insisting that all protein sources be lean (low-fat) as well as limited to no more than 3–4 ounces per serving (about the size of a deck of cards). This is in sharp contrast to many other low-carb plans, where carbohydrates are much more strictly limited than total fat, protein, or calories.

Zone dieters have to follow a lot of rules to attain this perfect balance of protein, fat, and carbohydrate at each meal, but the greater number and variety of carbo-hydrates allowed on this plan appeal to many. Carbohydrates like potatoes, pasta, and breads are classified as unfavorable carbohydrates, with consumption drastically reduced but never forbidden. As with other low-carb plans, insulin control is the primary goal, and all forms of sugar are discouraged, including artificial sweeteners.

Strict limits on consumption of red meat, egg yolks, and dairy fat can provide familiar and therefore comforting reassurance to dieters who may be apprehensive about other low-carb plans. I believe that the plan has merit and is greatly prefer-able over the current USDA food pyramid, but do feel that the relatively large amount of carbohydrates could induce cravings and problems with appetite control for those with severe intolerances to carbohydrates. It can also be very complicated to create your own meals and snacks that are perfectly balanced at the desired 40-40-30 ratio, so if you decide to try this plan, you would be well advised to purchase one of the many Zone cookbooks available.

The Zone
- Lower-fat and lower-calorie, with a lot more carbohydrates.
- Strict guidelines imposed on the precise balance of every meal and snack.
- Strict limit on consumption of red meat, dairy, and other saturated fats, with an emphasis on monounsaturated fats.
- Alcohol consumption discouraged but not forbidden, as long as it is accounted for in the 40-40-30 ratio.

Sugar Busters!

> *Leighton Steward, Morris Bethea, M.D., Sam Andrews, M.D., and Luis Balart, M.D.*

This plan relies heavily on the glycemic index, an oft-debated principle that rates the effects of specific foods on blood sugar. The creators of the index fed a group of control subjects precisely the same food, and then measured blood glucose levels afterward. The average reading following each food was then compared with the reading of a control food. Foods that cause larger average spikes in blood sugar are rated higher on the glycemic index than foods that do not affect blood sugar as much. Now, the key word to consider when discussing the glycemic index is *average*. Think about it for a minute. To even arrive at an average, you must first admit to the existence of extremes at both ends. What's to say that you might not end up being at one of the extremes? In that case, what good is the index to you?

This plan does not rely on complicated charts or an overload of information. Instead, the authors provide a clear and concise overview of their theory followed by a relatively simple chart and lists of foods to avoid and foods that are forbidden. They expound upon what foods you *can* eat, in far greater detail.

Some of the theories behind this diet contradict other plans of this nature. For instance, the Sugar Busters! authors believe that it is OK to eat fruit at all times when following this plan, but that fruit should always be eaten alone—either 30 minutes before or two hours after a meal. They allow fruit juice in the morning, theorizing that's OK because fluid empties more quickly from the stomach than solids and that fructose, the sugar in fruit, causes a significant release of insulin *only in the presence of previously elevated blood sugar*. Red wine is advised to be the best form of alcohol to indulge in, and beer the worst. Portions are strictly limited. Whole grains are allowed in more liberal quantities than in any other low-carb plan I have seen, leading some of the other plan authors to dismiss Sugar Busters! as not being low-carb at all.

Sugar Busters!

- Prohibits refined sugars but not those from fruit, as long as they're combined properly with other foods.
- Moderate fat consumption with emphasis on lean protein sources and portion control.
- Stresses glycemic index of foods more than carbohydrate count.
- Prohibits refined grains but allows relatively large quantities of whole unprocessed grains, whole-grain pasta, legumes, and brown and wild rice.
- Moderate alcohol consumption thought to be beneficial in proper combinations.

Neanderthin

> *Ray Audette*

Audette created his Paleolithic diet to improve his health. After suffering for years from rheumatoid arthritis, a painful autoimmune disorder, at the age of 34 he received the additional diagnosis of diabetes. Audette took matters into his own hands and headed to the library. His research resulted in many of the same conclusions as the foremost low-carb researchers of our day, and some that are unique to him. Following his plan eliminated any need for insulin injections, and his arthritis symptoms disappeared, too!

Neanderthin is the strictest of all low-carb plans, but the rules are easy to remember—in fact, there is only one: *If you were dropped off naked on the prehistoric tundra armed with nothing but a sharp stick and a rock (no fire), is this a food you could eat?* If yes, you may partake. If no, it is forbidden. There are no exceptions. In other words, if you couldn't eat it raw and without the intervention of technology, then you should never eat it—period. That rules out: all grains, all beans (fresh, dried, even coffee, and all legumes), all dairy products, all forms of sugar including honey and artificial sweeteners, all potatoes, and even a few gourds, nuts, and squash. Alcohol is off-limits, too.

Audette claims that all grains are "extremely carcinogenic" (cancer-causing), with corn considered the number one carcinogen in the American diet, responsible for more deaths than cigarettes. He points out that wild animals do not contract cancer—but our domesticated and beloved pets, whom we feed mostly grains, are rife with cancer and other diseases of civilization, just as we are. He makes a compelling case, but people most interested in weight loss will probably not be willing to make this drastic a change. If you are looking to improve your health, however, and are willing to follow this plan to the letter, it may the best hope you have.

Note that the plan allows fruits of all kinds, but it does point out that a portion of dried fruit should never exceed the amount you would have eaten were it still fresh, with juices limited the same way.

Neanderthin
- Completely prohibits all dairy, grains, beans, sugar, and alcohol for life.
- Allows all meats, fish, fresh fruits, and vegetables in almost unlimited quantity.
- Encourages ketosis for weight loss by eliminating all carbohydrates for a time and restricting others, as needed.

Somers's plan is mostly about food combining, while eliminating all foods she considers unnatural, and all highly processed foods. The gist is: Eat all foods in strict combinations. She says that proteins and fats are easily digested when eaten with vegetables only, but carbohydrates should be eaten only in their whole-grain form and without any fat at all. Foods that contain both carbohydrate and fat even in their natural state are considered unnatural or "funky," and are completely banned. This list includes nuts, avocados, and olives—foods rich in monounsaturated fats and encouraged in almost all other diets, even the lower-fat ones.

With "Somersizing," Somers has found a way to have her fruit and eat it, too, along with a dose of whole grain pasta when she wants, while maintaining that famous figure. But forget about whole-grain bagels with cream cheese, or chicken alfredo fettuccini, because of the "no fat with your carbs" rule. Granted, there is such a thing as fat-free cream cheese, but it consists mostly of chemicals with not much cheese, and Somers discourages eating any food that has been adulterated to that extent.

Somers's books are full of gourmet recipes, and she has some good advice on the emotional aspects of dieting.

Her theories on food combining are not well proved medically as of this date, and many of the doctors in this field refute the theory entirely. They argue that carbs should always, *always* be eaten with protein, because protein mitigates any sudden insulin release that fruit can trigger. But the Sugar Busters! authors and some other doctors are on Somers's side as far as the fruit-by-itself thing. In the absence of clearcut studies to support either assertion, and with thousands of people finding success food combining, it appears to be a viable plan for many.

Somersizing

- Eliminates sugars, highly starchy foods, caffeine, alcohol, and "funky foods" that combine fat and carbs, such as nuts, olives, liver, coconuts, soy, and all milks (cow, soy, rice).
- Allows cream and cheese.
- Allows fruits only when eaten alone, on an empty stomach.
- Allows proteins and fats to be eaten with vegetables, but not with carbs.
- Allows carbohydrates to be eaten with vegetables, but not with fat.

The Schwarzbein Principle

> *Diana Schwarzbein, M.D., and Nancy Deville*

Schwarzbein is a specialist in endocrinology, and she and her cowriter manage to explain very complicated medical subjects very clearly. I particularly recommend this diet plan to women, due to specific information included on menopausal issues and hormone replacement therapy. Schwarzbein also appears to have a good grasp of the emotional issues associated with obesity and weight loss.

This is another doctor who believes firmly that carbohydrates should always be eaten *with* protein. This diet advocates more carbohydrates than many of the other plans, on the principle that too few carbohydrates are just as bad as too many.

She agrees with many other low-carb advocates that cholesterol readings are not indicative of total health and should not be taken too seriously. Instead, she recommends that you ask yourself, "are you living a healthy life, or are you stressed, eating poorly, using stimulants and other drugs, and not exercising?"

Schwarzbein believes that dietary fat is vital, and that all fats found naturally in nature are good for us (saturated, monounsaturated, and polyunsaturated fats alike). She says our diets should be rich in fat and cholesterol from a variety of foods, such as avocados, butter, eggs, red meat, chicken, shellfish, olives, tofu, nuts, and seeds (since the only way to get the body to stop overproducing cholesterol on its own is to provide it with all it needs through diet).

This plan requires you to eliminate all caffeine and other stimulants, over-the-counter drugs, and sweeteners (both real and artificial), and to determine and eat the appropriate quantity of "real carbohydrates" (not man-made ones) that are appropriate for your individual activity level, current health, and metabolism. (Methods to determine this level are detailed.)

There are a ton of practical tips on shopping, cooking, eating out, and just plain coping in the book, plus a few recipes and lots of meal plans. There are companion cookbooks available as well.

Schwarzbein Principle
- Against ketosis.
- Allows more fats and more carbohydrates in the form of whole grains, fruits, vegetables.
- Bans sugars, artificial sweeteners, caffeine, alcohol, tobacco.
- Encourages specific natural hormone replacement therapy for women who need it.

The Carbohydrate Addict's Diet

> *Richard F. Heller. M.D., and Rachael F. Heller, M.D.*

Richard and Rachael Heller have written numerous books on their plan, including *The Carbohydrate Addict's Diet, The Carbohydrate Addict's Lifespan Program, The Carbohydrate Addict's Healthy Heart Program, Carbohydrate-Addicted Kids*, and *Healthy for Life*, plus several other companion works. *The Carbohydrate Addict's Diet*, however, is probably the best known of these books.

The Hellers created a unique program for curing insulin resistance and carbohydrate addiction. Their basic explanation for the cause of insulin resistance is similar to those in other plans, but they deviate greatly from other doctors in the way they choose to deal with it. They believe that people crave carbohydrates only when they have elevated insulin levels, and agree with the Sugar Busters! doctors in that they believe that insulin is only overproduced by the body when there are already-elevated levels. Their plan, therefore, allows for a daily "Reward Meal," when you are allowed to have *some* of absolutely any carbohydrate that you really want. You must adhere to very strict low-carb rules throughout the rest of the day, however, and portion control is a big part of this plan. No snacks are allowed between meals, and the Reward Meal must be strictly balanced between protein, fats, and carbs, as well as preceded by a large salad. (If you don't like salads and do enjoy snacking, you'll have a hard time following this one.) The Reward Meal must also end within one hour.

If you are disciplined enough to limit your portions and skip snacking, but desperately want to be able to eat (insert favorite carb here) occasionally without feeling guilty, then this plan could work for you.

The Carbohydrate Addict's Diet

- Allows any carbohydrate once per day as part of a strictly balanced reward meal, including some alcohol.
- Limits all other carbohydrates throughout the day and allows no snacks between meals.

GO-Diet

> *Jack Goldberg, Ph.D., and Karen O'Mara, D.O.*

This plan stresses the consumption of lots of fiber and low carbs, with daily ingestion of yogurt, buttermilk, or kefir. These authors believe that the active cultures in fermented milk products are crucial to maintaining balance in the intestinal tract, and made the assertion back in 1999 that the carbs in yogurt should be counted as less than the total carbs stated on the label, a practice just now being adopted by some manufacturers.

This plan counts "net carbs" as total carbohydrates less fiber and asks you to ingest at least 25 grams of fiber each day from vegetables, fruits, nuts, and sources such as bran, flax seed, and psyllium seed. Whole grains are not encouraged but can make up part of the under-50-per-day net carb allotment. Alcohol is allowed in moderation, including light beer.

Forbidden foods include sugar, milk, all forms of potatoes, all forms of beans with the exception of green pole beans, turnips, rice, lentils, corn, peas, high-carb fruits, and flour. Allowed foods include lean meats, fish, cheese, heavy cream, sour cream, eggs, vegetables, nuts, seeds, and the lower-carb fruits.

Total fat and calories are not limited, but they do want saturated fat kept as low as possible and monounsaturated fats to make up 50% of the total. Ketosis is explained as beneficial and the cause for weight loss and increased energy levels, but unlike some plans that strive for ketosis, this one specifically discourages the use of ketone strips, saying they measure only one type of ketone when two can be produced, and the only real test for ketosis is successful weight loss.

The food list in the GO-Diet plan is limited, but you are allowed to eat anytime you are hungry, and portions of the allowed foods are not limited except by carb count.

GO-Diet

- High-fiber, low-carb, encourages ketosis and daily yogurt products.
- Allows alcohol in moderation.
- Encourages high monounsaturated and low saturated fat.
- Strict limits on food types, with generous portions.

Life Without Bread

> *Christian B. Allan, Ph.D., and Wolfgang Lutz, M.D.*

This is another diet that is very easy to follow, with a bare minimum of rules, boiling down to this: *Eat no more than 72 carbohydrates per day.* Period. That's it. No net carbs, no restrictions on fat or calories, just the restriction on total carbs (with a caveat about avoiding the typical "bad" carbs).

The authors explain the biological processes of normal cells, bacteria, viruses, enzymes, hormones, and cancer cells very well, and they draw a clear and detailed picture of the connection between our typical high-carb Western diet and the many modern diseases of humans, particularly, but certainly not limited to, cancer.

This doctor says a few things that will surprise many—like the fact that saturated fat is actually the most stable kind and is very good for you! That your heart cannot even beat without it. And that high cholesterol levels in the blood have never been proved to correlate with death rates. To the contrary, he says, most patients who die of severe heart disease have relatively normal cholesterol levels. Would you be as shocked as I was to learn that a coroner's study from 1990 found that in deceased people with the most severe heart disease, the average cholesterol level was just 186? This book contains a wealth of such research.

Life Without Bread theorizes that higher levels of LDL cholesterol are not unhealthy because it is only high homocysteine levels in the blood that make the LDL protein adhere to the arterial walls. They say that high homocysteine levels occur because of a deficiency in three vitamins: B6, B12, and folic acid, all of which can be found in abundant quantity in ... drum roll, please ... saturated fat, animal foods, and leafy veggies—the backbone of low-carb eating.

Anyone interested in low-carb diets for health reasons should check out this plan, even if they decide to ultimately follow another plan.

Life Without Bread
- Limits carb consumption to less than 72 grams per day for life.
- Does not limit total fat, saturated fat, or calories.
- Allows moderate alcohol consumption.
- Explains ketosis as beneficial and nothing to fear, but not a usual result of this diet.

Your Fat Can Make You Thin

> *Calvin Ezrin, M.D.*

This diet plan is both low-carb and low-calorie, with an emphasis on ketosis. Daily use of "ketostix" to measure the ketones in your urine is a requirement, as well as very specific supplements. One of the recommended therapies during the weight loss portion of the diet includes small doses of a prescription drug (tradazone) to improve serotonin levels. Thus, you will need the cooperation of a physician to follow this plan.

You will also need an iron will, to comply with narrow dietary restrictions of fewer than 40 carbs per day with no added fat or oil of any kind, and a daily limit of 800–1200 total calories. In sharp contrast to most other low-carb diets, on this one protein is very restricted, with women being advised to limit their intake to 7 ounces per day in addition to one egg *or* two ounces of cottage cheese. (Men are allowed slightly more than that, but not much.) The author assures us that the carb restrictions will reduce appetite sufficiently to ensure success without duress. Artificial sweeteners are allowed with sugar-free gelatin mentioned often in the menus as an option.

The technical portions of this book could very well result in a loud whooshing sound as most of it flies right over your head, but to the good doctor's credit the summaries that follow these passages are easily understood. (Besides, that local physician you are going to need may just benefit from the inclusion of those passages.)

Long-term carb restriction is not advocated, with the emphasis remaining on calories. Saturated fat should compose no more than 10 percent of total calories, with long-term goals of 30 percent of calories from fat, 40–50 percent from carbohydrate, and 20–30 percent from protein. (You can pretty much say good-bye to red meat and almost all dairy products if you choose this plan.)

Your Fat Can Make You Thin
- Low-fat, low-calorie, and low-carb with strict ban on saturated fats.
- Requires prescription drug therapy during weight loss phase only.
- Bans alcohol during weight loss phase; allowed in moderation on maintenance.
- Returns all forms of carbs to the diet after weight loss, with continued calorie restrictions.

The Insulin Resistance Diet

> *Cheryle R. Hart M.D., Mary Kay Grossman, R.D.*

This book advertises itself as a way to discover if "insulin resistance is the culprit for those extra pounds" and to enjoy "good health without fad dieting." It advocates much higher levels of carbohydrates than other plans, with an emphasis on low-fat foods in combination with "adequate protein," defined as 40–70 grams per day for most people, not to exceed 90 grams per day even in an extreme athlete. Total fat is only 30 percent of total calories, in line with non-low-carb diets. There are no forbidden foods on this plan (except fatty ones). While you're allowed almost unlimited dairy products on this plan, said dairy products must all be low-fat, or, better yet, non-fat versions, as well as sugar-free. For each 15 grams of carbohydrate consumed, you must consume a minimum of 7 grams of protein, a process the authors call "linking." They say linking works because mixing protein with other foods counteracts and lowers insulin's reaction to those other foods (another vote against food-combining).

At one point these authors say, "High insulin levels also interfere with the kidneys' ability to clear uric acid from the body." They go on to say that high levels of uric acid result in gout and kidney stones, as well as coronary heart disease. Now, that's refreshing—someone claiming that a *high-carbohydrate* diet results in gout and kidney stones!

They discuss the benefits of mono and polyunsaturated fats rather intelligibly, versus the dangers of free radicals and trans-fatty acids, but nevertheless limit nuts and other acknowledged "good oils" to a total of 4 tablespoons per day. They recommend margarine and liquid fat substitutes throughout the book, even after discussing thoroughly the dangers of trans-fatty acids, a contradiction that is exacerbated further in the book's recipes, which don't seem to fit the authors' own linking formula. The book includes some questionable (to this author) passages on the dangers of ketogenic diets that seem to confuse benign dietary ketosis with diabetic ketoacidosis (more on that issue on page 30).

The Insulin Resistance Diet

- Allows higher levels of carbs from all sources, even refined ones, as long as eaten with adequate protein.
- Vehemently opposed to ketosis, which they appear to confuse with ketoacidosis.
- Total calories and fat extremely limited, emphasis on polyunsaturated and monounsaturated sources.
- Alcohol limited to 8 ounces per week.

The South Beach Diet

> *Arthur Agatston, M.D.*

This "new" diet hit the scene in 2004 promising normal-size helpings of protein from all sources, plenty of vegetables, eggs, cheese, nuts, salads with real oil in the dressing, regular snacks, and even dessert after dinner—all that during the strictest phase. Fruit, pasta, rice, bread, potatoes, and the like are completely off-limits for the first two weeks, considered "Phase I," but immediately after that, South Beach dieters are encouraged to reintroduce small amounts of the less refined and carb-laden versions of these foods on a regular basis (while testing their reaction and adjusting intake accordingly). Dairy products are limited, with reduced or non-fat versions encouraged. Canola, olive, and soy oils are preferred to butter. Leaner cuts of meat are emphasized, but steak is still on the menu. Bacon is frowned upon in favor of its less fatty cousin, Canadian bacon, but still permitted. Nuts are limited to single portions such as 15 almonds, precisely counted out, or 30 pistachios. All forms of beans (legumes) are allowed.

The final phase of the diet, maintenance, is the most liberal, when Agatston says you can forget all but the most basic rules and need only return to the stricter version if you gain back weight. In comparison with other low-carb diets, this one is more liberal than most as far as carbohydrate consumption, more strict than many about total fat consumption, and in sharp contrast to a few other plans as far as which foods and fats are healthy and which are not.

Due to a slightly more moderate approach to fat coupled with a very hefty ad budget, the South Beach Diet managed to rapidly convert many former low-carb skeptics. I find that somewhat amusing, since apart from the restriction on saturated fat (still a controversial subject in this field that has yet to be proved as medically necessary in combination with a low-carb regime) and an occasionally more relaxed attitude about real sugars, it is not much different than the original Atkins or Protein Power diets. I guess it's true when they say, "Timing is everything."

The South Beach Diet

- Lower fat and lower calorie, with more carbohydrates in the form of fruit, grains, and dried beans.
- Allows small amounts of real sugar and foods like white potatoes that are mostly forbidden on other plans.
- No alcohol during Phase I, allowed in moderation (preferably red wine) after that—but you should say good-bye to beer—light, low-carb, or otherwise.

Beyond Atkins

> *Douglas J. Markham, M.D.*

This author trademarked the phrase "The Healthier Than Atkins Diet" for the cover of his book. Markham calls this the Total Health Program and can count both John Schneider and Larry King among his high-profile converts.

His main message is simple: increase protein and decrease "bad carbohydrates." He advises his patients to always eat protein with carbs (yet another vote against the Somersizing and Sugar Busters! methods of food-combining). He relies on the glycemic index (which I discuss in Sugar Busters! on page 17) to determine good carbs as opposed to bad ones. He reduces fat consumption by type also, labeling saturated bad and monounsaturated good. The biggest difference between his plan and Atkins appears to be the fat restrictions and the fact that he encourages more fruit intake to avoid the still-controversial state of ketosis.

Markham seems to suggest that ketosis is not dangerous when he says, "Unless one is an insulin-dependent diabetic or literally starving to death due to a lack of food, there is little to no danger from ketosis which is not characterized by a simultaneous rise in blood glucose and blood acidity." However, he later parrots the age-old kidney-damage myths. "The by-product of burning fat is ketones, which accumulate in the body and pass through our kidneys before being excreted in the urine. This is thought to be potentially damaging to the kidneys." These messages clearly contradict each other and could potentially be confusing to a reader who is seeking clarity on the ketosis safety issue.

Markham advocates use of artificial sweeteners and includes a good rundown on the various kinds. His meal plans include things like protein bars, and he gives the OK to deduct all fiber, sugar alcohols, and other ingredients currently discounted by manufacturers on food labels ("net" carbs). The daily protein requirements listed in this book appear to exactly match those given in the 1995 version of *Protein Power*, and his meal plans for the weight loss phase seem to average ten grams of carbohydrates per meal, also exactly as in *Protein Power*. Maybe he should have called this book *Beyond Protein Power* instead?

Beyond Atkins

- Allows more "good" carbs and fruit than some other low-carb diets.
- Restricts "bad" fats and encourages portion control.
- Allows artificial sweeteners and convenience-type snacks and foods.
- Allows alcohol in moderation when combined with protein; pure spirits preferred.

The Hamptons Diet

> *Fred Pescatore, M.D.*

The latest offering from this former medical director of the Atkins Center may be his best work yet, at least from a reading standpoint. This one is a little lighter on the actual science (the part that goes right over most readers' heads anyway) and much heavier on the simply explained how-tos (the part the average reader benefits from the most). Earlier works include *Thin for Good, Feed Your Kids Well*, and *The Allergy and Asthma Cure.*

The basic low-carb, moderate-fat diet originally outlined in *Thin for Good* hasn't changed a whole lot. Pescatore explains that where he differs from Dr. Atkins is in the amount and type of fats he recommends, not the basic principles. The Hamptons Diet prescribes regular use of macadamia nut oil, in the place of all other choices. Because macadamia nut oil contains equally balanced omega-3 and omega-6 fats and is also the richest in monounsaturated omega-9 fats, with a high smoke point, he says it is by far the healthiest choice for everyone.

This book presents several new food pyramids that will help you make wise food choices from each food category. This is an original strategy that should be a very useful diet aid.

One of Pescatore's strongest consistent messages, for which he has earned my utmost respect, is that we should all be eating real food—the less processed and the less manipulated, the better. He warns to never eat trans fats, margarine, hydrogenated fats, or—this will be surprising to some—canola oil (completely man-made, and highly refined.) He refers specifically to protein shakes, bars, and most commercially produced low-carb snack foods as "crutches." He states unequivocally that there is no such thing as a "net" carbohydrate, and while still encouraging high fiber, he says the only number that counts on any label is the total carb count. He encourages organics, while recognizing that not everyone will be able to afford to eat organically all the time, including himself. It appears that even if his body is in the Hamptons most of the time these days, his wallet has remained firmly in middle America.

The Hamptons Diet

- Specifies use of macadamia nut oil in place of all other oils and encourages organic foods.
- Restricts total carb intake according to weight loss or maintenance phase, with no truly forbidden foods.
- Includes several clever new food pyramids.
- Encourages moderate alcohol consumption.

Part 2

Low-Carb Myths Debunked

Myth: Ketosis is dangerous

> *The confusion with ketoacidosis*

K etoacidosis can occur when a Type I diabetic has a toxic buildup of blood glucose due to a complete absence of insulin, and yes, it does result in muscle and tissue breakdown, and it is often deadly. Ketoacidosis can also occur when an individual is literally starving to death, as the body breaks down existing muscle tissue and cannibalizes itself.

Benign dietary ketosis occurs when there are insufficient carbohydrates present to convert to glucose and meet the body's immediate energy needs. In most people that occurs at least once a day, during sleep, regardless of how many carbohydrates they routinely ingest. When insufficient carbohydrates are present to meet immediate energy needs, the body's best option is to break down existing fat tissue and turn it into ketones, which the body easily and efficiently uses for energy needs. In fact, studies have shown that the heart and brain both function 25 percent more efficiently on ketones than they do on pure glucose! As long as you are consuming sufficient protein when limiting carbs, your body will not break down muscle mass during this process.

Ketones are a natural by-product of fat burning: *any* fat burning—body fat or even dietary fat that you eat. The same holds true for alcohol—consume too much and ketones will be produced since it is the alcohol burning, not body fat. When you produce more ketones than the body needs at that time for energy, the extra ketones are excreted both through urine and respiration. They pass through the kidneys first, and it has been theorized that this may irritate the kidneys, but this theory has never been proved in any medical study .

When ketones are excreted through respiration, they can cause bad breath, often referred to as "keto breath." This is probably the worst side effect of ketosis, but it is hardly dangerous.

Myth: You must measure for ketones

> *You may want to, but you don't have to*

You do not necessarily need to measure for ketones, even when ketosis is desirable. While some plans call for you to measure ketones (by testing your urine), the best measure of success for any diet has got to be actual weight loss (or health improvement, if you are not dieting for weight loss).

Now, *this part is really important*, so listen up: Even a person who is in ketosis might not register positive for ketones on the test strips, because the body produces two types of ketones, and the test strips detect only one of them.

The second reason the strips are not very useful in the real world is that ketones are the by-product of burning fat—but whether it happens to be dietary or body fat doesn't matter; that doesn't affect the ketones or the readings. So, if you are eating lots of dietary fat and burning that for energy instead of body fat, you can and will produce ketones whether you are burning any body fat or not. Thus, you can register positive for ketones on the strips and still not lose any weight.

TIP: *Most of the time, ketosis is plainly evident by the metallic taste it causes in one's mouth.*

Myth: A calorie is a calorie is a calorie

> Not all calories are created equal

We have heard it so often that most of us could probably recite it in our sleep: "The only way to lose weight is to burn more calories than you eat." Critics of low-carb diets usually take a step further, and claim: "If low-carb diets work, it's only because people on low-carb diets eat fewer calories overall, since low-carb diets suppress the appetite." To that I can only say: "So? What's your point? We eat as much as we want, we are satisfied with our food, and we are losing weight. What's wrong with that, even if it's true?"

Well, as it happens, it is not true! A study published by Harvard University in early 2004 surprised a lot of people (www.news.harvard.edu/gazette/2003/10.23/03-lowcarb.html). In this study, low-carb dieters lost more weight than low-fat dieters, despite eating 300 additional calories each day over a 12-week study period. That's a total of 25,000 extra calories per person! And they lost more weight—not the same amount, but more. Kind of stands the calorie-is-a-calorie-is-a-calorie theory on its head, doesn't it?

My own experience backs this up. I had a hard time losing weight on a very low-carb diet until I increased the fat percentage in my diet. It didn't make a lot of sense to me then, but I was tracking every bite I ate in a nutritional program that broke everything down for me, and cutting back on those things certainly didn't help. Increasing my fat and calories was something I tried as a last resort, and I admit to being pretty shocked when it worked.

Please realize that this may not be the case for everyone, and it can change over time. When you reach maintenance, calories may matter more. That could be due to the increased carbs most of us eat once we declare ourselves on maintenance, or it might just be due to the body's ability to adapt to any routine over time. Regardless, I know for a fact that I eat more food now (way more calories and fat than I used to before I went low-carb) while easily maintaining my weight loss.

Myth: Low-carb eating is not balanced

Any eating plan can be unbalanced, including the average diet of most of America. How many people do you know that actually eat six or more servings each day of fruits and vegetables? Not many, I would wager!

The plan recommendations all include real foods, lots of them, and lots of high-fiber vegetables and fruits. Just because we tend to not eat a few of the highest-carb veggies and fruits doesn't mean we are eating none. The idea is low-carb, not no-carb! Sugar, flour, potatoes and corn never balanced any diet—cutting those out of or reducing them in anyone's diet is never a bad thing.

The important thing to remember is this: Make *wise* and *conscious* carb choices at all times—not obsessive ones. Don't fall into the trap of thinking that the lower your carbs, the better you are doing. Just because you *can* subsist on nothing but meat does not mean that you should!

I have analyzed my dietary intake over a long period of time, and *surprise, surprise!* Come to find out, I am getting at least the RDA (recommended daily allowance) just from my diet in everything that has an established recommendation. The only thing that went off the chart even a little is my sodium level, higher than recommended, and I am not in the least concerned about that since my cardiac risk assessment tests are in the normal range now.

Myth: Low-carb eating will raise your cholesterol

In most cases, nothing could be further from the truth. The fastest way to raise your total blood cholesterol appears to be following the current USDA food pyramid and limiting your dietary cholesterol. Our bodies make cholesterol for a reason—it is necessary for life. Without cholesterol, your cells cannot function. Limiting cholesterol in the diet just causes the body to produce more on its own.

Many physicians think it is the *ratio* of the different kinds of cholesterol in your blood that matters most. The real problem with cholesterol appears to have more to do with the structure of LDL cholesterol particles (commonly known as the "bad" cholesterol) and other things in the blood that doctors had not even identified back in the day when they started telling people to cut down on the cholesterol that they were eating. These things include C-reactive protein and homocysteine, and you can learn a lot more about them in many of the low-carb books I've discussed here.

Triglycerides may actually be a far better indicator of coronary risk than LDL. High triglycerides in conjunction with low HDL (the "good" cholesterol) is the combination that appears to be most deadly. This just happens to be the ratio that low-carb eating improves most, in most people.

LDL cholesterol level tests are misleading, since there are two distinctly different particle structures that LDL can have, and standard tests can only show total levels, not the size or makeup of the particles present. People who have high triglycerides tend to form LDL particles that are small and dense and are capable of slipping under the lining of arteries to form the plaque that can clog them. People who eat low-carb tend to have lower triglyceride levels and tend to form large LDL particles that do not have that same tendency. When you successfully change the makeup of LDL particles, tests can show a higher level than before, even if the number of total particles is lower, because the size of each particle is so much greater. This can account for a rise in the LDL levels in some low-carb dieters.

TIP:

Even experts do not agree on optimal cholesterol levels. I have spoken with physicians and read as much on this issue as I can, and have chosen to trust the judgments of those experts whose opinions make the most sense to me. I have presented to you here my reasoned perspective as to the validity of the opinions I have chosen to rely on. Only you can and should make these kinds of informed decisions in regard to your own life. I urge you to talk to your physician(s) and decide how to proceed.

Part 3

Eight Things You Should Do—and Two You Shouldn't—on Any Low-Carb Diet

DO: Drink lots of water

There are a multitude of reasons for this good advice, and it is universally accepted as a good idea no matter what else you do in life—there's no controversy here! There are some reasons why it is more important than ever to drink enough water when leading a low-carb lifestyle, however.

First is the ketone issue. When you are in ketosis and producing ketones, they can cause some really bad breath. Drinking sufficient amounts of water will dilute the ketones and prevent this from getting out of hand, not to mention that it will make the metallic taste in your mouth less noticeable.

Second, if you don't drink enough water, your body will compensate by retaining more water! That can affect your weight on the scale, as well as how you look.

Third, sometimes when you feel hungry, it is really your body crying out for water, not food. So drinking water can also help you alleviate hunger pangs.

Last and perhaps most important is this: Lack of sufficient water intake will slow down your metabolism and make you feel tired. Slowing down your metabolism is the last thing you want when you are trying to lose weight, and feeling tired is something no one wants, ever.

Drinking up to a gallon of water per day seems impossible at first, but cutting out things like soda and juice can help a lot. I use a one-liter bottle for tracking my water intake each day. I have four lines painted on the bottle, and an elastic band that I move down one line each time I refill the bottle. I don't always make it to the number four line, but most of the time I do—and when I don't, I can really feel the difference in my energy level.

DO: Exercise!

I used to think exercise was a dirty word. I love to play sports but I hate to just exercise. If there's a ball I want to catch, I will run. Getting me fired up about walking or running for its own sake is pretty tough, though. But exercise is necessary to succeed with weight loss.

Yes, you can lose 50 or 100 or even 200 pounds without exercising. But if you want to look good when you are done losing, you had better make an effort to tone what you've got left! Your skin is much more likely to shrink back into shape when you lose weight in combination with exercise, and your metabolism will definitely improve.

Let's be brutally honest here—those of us with lots of weight to lose most likely have somewhat addictive personalities, anyway. Why not put that trait to work for us this time? Exercise is as addicting as anything else, and much more rewarding. I walked my butt off—literally. This diet would not have worked for me without adding exercise. Some people lose weight just fine with no exercise, but other people do not. Luckily, I came to enjoy my walking so much that it is no longer just exercise but has become "me time." It is something I get to do, all by myself, three times a week, and I don't feel guilty for taking the time for myself. I feel better each time after finishing, and let's fact it, a happy mommy is a much better mommy...and wife!

After the first couple months of walking, I added wrist and leg weights, along with some weight lifting for my triceps, biceps, and pecs. Eventually I even found my abs and incorporated crunches.

TIP: *Find some sort of exercise that you can enjoy, or at least consider doing, and incorporate it into your life. Pretty soon it will become second nature to you, and even if you never really come to enjoy it, you will stop hating it!*

DO: Take good-quality supplements regularly

> You won't regret it

Even though a thorough analysis of my low-carb diet showed that I was already getting the RDA of the recognized important vitamins and minerals, I still take supplements regularly. For one thing, the RDA for most vitamins is considered woefully inadequate by many experts, and for another, there are a lot of things that the RDA does not address—including timing. Unless you get certain things in the proper combinations, the presence or absence of other things can hinder or even block their absorption. Any excess will simply be eliminated by the body, so with a few exceptions it is hard to take too much of most of them.

There is no official recommendation for essential fatty acid (EFA) supplementation, yet most experts agree on the importance of balancing the omega-3 and omega-6 fats that we eat, as well as getting enough monounsaturated fat. This is another instance of ratios being far more important than overall quantity. Something important to consider, however, is that in the case of essential fatty acids, taking poor-quality supplements can be worse for your health than not taking them at all. Omega-3 fatty acids, the kind found in fish and flax seeds and the kind that most of us do not get enough of, are the most unstable of all—meaning if they are not manufactured, handled, and stored properly, they can go rancid. When they turn rancid, they go from being a good thing to being an actively dangerous substance. In *Protein Power Lifeplan*, the Eadeses cite studies where researchers tested bottles of fish-oil capsules from the shelves of health-food stores and found that almost 50 percent of the time, at least *some* of the capsules in any given bottle were rancid. Yet getting enough fish oil from natural sources can put you in danger of getting too much mercury. It's enough to make anyone's head spin!

I'd like to give you an ironclad list of dos and don'ts for supplementation, but there are so many variables involved that even if I did, someone else's advice would be sure to contradict mine. This is another area in which you really need to do your own research (including, as always, consulting your physician). One of the best books I have read on this is *Dr. Atkins' Vita-Nutrient Solution*. I do urge you to incorporate, at the very minimum, a complete multivitamin (which might or might not include iron and calcium, depending on lots of individual factors) plus some EFAs. Potassium is crucial for most people at the beginning, at least, but do refer back to "When you start a low-carb diet," on page 10, for some important cautions.

DO: Keep a food diary

> And keep it honest

Studies show that people who keep an *honest* food diary are much more likely to be successful losing weight. I know it helped me, because I had to tweak what I was doing to find the right combination of things that worked best for me. Things become clear on a graph after three months of plotting the ups and downs in your weight and the corresponding food intake. There are many software programs out there that can help you do this easily. You can plug in what you eat and drink, and the program will tell you exactly how many carbs, calories, and so on, were in them.

You don't have to use a computer to count carbs and what-not, of course. But doing so will help you avoid many common "hidden carbs" in foods you might have thought were "free." (Not much in this life is *really* free—is it?)

Often a label states 0 carbs per serving when there are actually quite a few carbs in a realistic-size serving of the food! As a dedicated low-carb eater, make it your business to know whether a label is correct as written, or not. *You won't believe how often the answer is not.*

For any product that claims 0 carbs, you can check it by noting the calories and then adding up the fat and protein calories. If there are calories left over and there is sugar, corn syrup, dextrose, fructose, or any other "ose" (except for sucralose or cellulose gum) in the ingredients, it is in all likelihood a hidden carb of the very worst kind.

Warning: In my experience, sugar alcohol carbs seem to cause people the most problems—I suggest you use these products with great caution during active weight loss and omit them entirely at the beginning. They are a great occasional treat, and used in moderation they can make maintenance a real pleasure. But they play havoc with the formula above, and they can play havoc with weight loss as well.

TIP: *Sugar alcohols (artificial sweeteners also known as polyols) are not counted like other carbs. Manufacturers are permitted under current FDA rulings to determine their own nutritional information for these sweeteners, which can vary widely. Most do not have 4 calories per gram of carbohydrate; some have only 2; some even less. Some low-carb diet plans permit you to subtract these carbs from your daily count. Manufacturers must by law list them accurately. They usually claim "net" or "effective" carb counts prominently somewhere outside the nutrition data label.*

Hidden Carbs Formula

Heavy whipping cream, per label:

- Serving size: 1 tablespoon
- 60 calories per serving
- 6 grams of fat
- 0 grams of protein

- 0 grams of carbohydrate
- Fat = 9 calories per gram
- Protein and carbohydrates = 4 calories per gram

Do the Math:

6 x 9 = 54 calories

0 x 4 = 0 calories

0 x 4 = 0 calories

Total: 54 calories

As you can see, there are 6 calories unaccounted for. It's unknown what they are from, but there's a good chance those extra calories come from carbs, and in cream, they do. Actual carbohydrate count for 1 cup of heavy whipping cream at 38 percent butterfat is 6.6 carbs, or 0.41 per tablespoon. Because it is less than 0.5 carbs per serving, the manufacturers are allowed to round it down to 0 when it is obviously not 0. These carbs can really add up if you eat a whole cup of a food like that.

Other Common Hidden Carbs

- Large eggs: 0.6 grams each
- Spices: For example, for onion and garlic powders, the label states that one serving equals 1/2 teaspoon, for 0 carbs. According to the USDA, garlic powder has 2.036 carbs per teaspoon, and onion powder has 1.694 carbs per teaspoon. Big difference!
- Artificial sweeteners: Packets claim 0 carbs, at 2 servings each, but they are usually 0.9 grams per packet.
- Brewed coffee: Contains 0.8 grams per 6 ounce cup. Note that an average coffee mug actually holds 9–12 ounces.
- Sugar-free powdered drink mixes: Five calories per 8 ounces would equal 1.25 grams of carbohydrates, yet most labels say zero. Two quarts equal 10 grams— again, big difference!

DO: Be a smart medical consumer

If you made it this far and you are still reading, you have already started educating yourself about low-carb eating. Don't stop here! Keep reading. Keep asking questions, and keep applying common-sense logic to the answers you are offered. Knowledge is power—arm yourself with as much as you can. Choose a doctor who is willing to work with you, and be sure to have diagnostic medical tests performed regularly (before and during the diet).

If your doctor isn't willing to support you in trying this way of eating, it may be time to find a new one. The family doctor I used for many, many years counseled me about my out-of-control weight for years, then when my triglycerides went up over 400, he sent me to a dietitian for low-fat diet coaching and put me on Lipitor, a statin drug designed to lower cholesterol. After five months of miserable low-fat dieting and regular exercise plus the drug, they took another test that indicated that my triglycerides alone were somewhere over 1000. But what they really said was that they were way too high to measure accurately, completely off the charts. Then they told me they wanted me to start taking another drug, Lopid. Incredulously, I asked, "Why? Because the first one worked so well?"

Now, I am not telling you to ignore the advice of your physician. I am telling you to find a physician with an open mind. It only took eight weeks on a low-carb diet for my triglycerides to drop to under 100 and my total cholesterol to under 200—the quintessential "normal." When I saw those first test results, I literally burst into tears. When I told the doctor (a new one) how I had finally gotten my cholesterol under control, he was astounded. Shocked, even. But even though he thought he was dead-set against low-carb diets, after comparing the lab results in my file, he told me, "Just keep doing whatever you're doing, because it is obviously working!"

My total cholesterol eventually ended up stabilizing around 240. My LDL is a little higher than my doctor would like, but my good HDL cholesterol level is great, finally, and my triglycerides are still under control after 4½ years. Nothing else ever helped at all. I feel confident that controlling health conditions through dietary means is the first and best way, and my lab tests prove beyond any doubt that low-carb is the very best diet for me.

DO: Find some kind of outside support

It is tough to go it alone. Especially if you are the only one in your family eating a certain way. We all need support. There are many ways to get support for your low-carb lifestyle, including online message groups and chat rooms, community support groups, and diet and exercise buddies.

Being able to ask questions, share your triumphs, and vent your inevitable frustrations really can make all the difference. Low-carb was much less well-known when I started, and local support groups didn't exist in my small town, certainly. I found the support I needed online initially, and went on from there to create my own Web site and a new career.

Start by searching for the official Web site for the plan you've decided to follow. I have listed many of those at the end of this book, in Part 5: Additional Resources. In many cases, these sites list additional support resources. If you don't like the online message forum at one site, find another—there are millions of them out there, a sure sign that they are helpful. Policies vary widely from one to another, however, so it may be a good idea to observe for a while before you jump right in to participate.

TIP: *Check local papers, bulletin boards, and resource lists for support groups. If you don't find one in your area, consider starting one yourself. Most communities have some kind of facility that groups of this kind can use for free or for a nominal fee.*

DO: Resist negative pressure from family or friends

> *A lesson in putting yourself first*

I firmly believe that you must at certain times in life put yourself first. *This is not necessarily a selfish act, and it is no reason to feel guilty.* If you always put yourself last, continually bowing to the wishes of others, attending only to their needs, worrying only about their feelings, acquiescing only to their wishes, then no matter how much you love these people, eventually you may come to feel as though as you have no control over anything. This in itself is a surefire recipe for depression, and depression is one of the most common reasons mentioned for overeating and binge eating.

Now, please, I am not telling you to go out and do whatever you want, whenever you want. But I am saying: *Take that bubble bath once in a while!* The dust will still be there tomorrow, I promise. If your spouse doesn't enjoy the kind of movies that you do, throw caution to the wind and go without him or her once in a while! And I am also, especially, saying this: No matter how out-of-control your life feels, no matter how unfair, how unjust, how sad, how happy, no matter where you are or what you are doing, there is at least one thing that you can almost always control, at all times, barring being stranded on a desert island. You know where I am going with this, right? There is no one out there, now that you are an adult, including your mommy, who should be able to influence something as basic as what you do and do not choose to put in your mouth! And they shouldn't feel the need to try!!

That word I used, *choose?* It is an important one. You need to remember that you can eat anything. Of course you can! But you *choose* not to, right now.

Never tell yourself that you "can't eat that," because that might make you feel deprived or somehow cheated. Instead, tell yourself and others that you "choose not to eat that today." Keep uppermost in your mind at all time what is most important. It's not like you don't know what birthday cake tastes like, or are in danger of forgetting anytime soon. And your not eating someone else's birthday treat is not going to cause rain to fall on their parade.

TIP:

Tell anyone who insists that you eat something you shouldn't or don't want, "I know you love me and so you must want me to feel good and be healthy more than you want me to eat that."

DO: Follow your plan religiously

One of the best ways to make sure that you get the most out of any eating plan is to concentrate on eating only "healthy carbs." Concentrate on getting your daily allotment of carbs only from fruits, vegetables, legumes, nuts, seeds, dairy foods, and very limited amounts of whole grains. One carb is not just like another. Simply limiting your daily carbs to a certain number is not enough. Instead, you should try to space out your carbs throughout the day, and you should never eat anything with real sugar, honey, corn syrup, cornstarch, or refined flour in it if you can possibly help it. Even if these no-nos are present in a small enough percentage to make the stated serving equal just one carb, most of the time here in the real world, people eat much more than the suggested serving. You may be able to stick to your daily carb allotment eating regular ketchup on your burgers, or eating convenience foods made with *just a little* refined flour, or even sauces made with cornstarch, but these foods can and do cause cravings, and even if you resist those, you will not be doing yourself any favors in the long run. It is far better to modify the original behavior (or food) than to obsess over restricting food quantities. Foods that contain trace amounts of these ingredients can be used in moderation, especially when they are diluted by being used as an ingredient, as in the case of soy or Worcestershire sauce—but for best health and weight loss results, I recommend that this practice be the exception and not the rule.

The authors of some diet plans don't understand any of this—they just think that when people eat fewer than some number of grams of carbs per day, they will lose weight. In many of their suggested meal plans, they propose eating ridiculous servings of high-glycemic high-carb foods as side dishes—such as a quarter cup of mashed potatoes, two tablespoons of corn, or a quarter of a biscuit. Sure, I can really see me doing that anytime soon. (Not!! Ever heard of the word *tease?*)

TIP: *Even if the plan you choose says you can occasionally eat your old favorites and then get back on track, don't believe it.*

DO NOT: Put too much emphasis on your scale weight

> *Scales don't tell the whole story*

Scales lie! Seriously, they are notoriously bad indicators of progress—especially for low-carb dieters, who tend to weigh more because they have more lean mass. A person's weight can fluctuate by as much as 7 pounds in a day just from water fluctuations!

Then there's the fact that most of us are extremely protein deficient when we first begin eating this way. For years, we heard that eggs and red meat are bad for you and you should never eat more than a serving the size of a deck of cards, and so on. Then suddenly we start giving our bodies all the raw material (protein) it wants. *Woo-whee!* the body says. *I better latch on to this stuff and use it to make some new muscle—who knows when I will have it this good again?* Well, muscle weighs a lot more than fat—but it is much smaller, and it looks a whole lot better on. So do yourself a favor, and take your measurements regularly. Easier than that, keep a pair of too-small jeans around the house, and try them on each week. The day you can pull them up over your hips will be a proud day indeed. The day when you can actually zip them, you'll probably dance a jig.

It is common that when people first start eating low-carb, they lose quite a good amount of weight in the first two weeks. About week three, however, they may experience a stall on the scale while their body catches up to such a big change. My own such stall lasted for over a month. Now, during all that time, the scale didn't budge, but to my great surprise, I lost a whole bunch of inches. Had I gotten frustrated or disgusted and gone off plan, I would never have realized how much actual progress I was still making!

TIP: *Stop thinking of low-carb as a temporary diet, and start thinking of it as just the way you eat, instead—a lifestyle—and your patience level should go way up.*

DO NOT: Eat a bunch of low-carb "junk"

> *The diet won't work*

They say repetition is the best way to get someone to remember something, so even though I said this already, just a few pages back, here it comes again: Concentrate on eating only healthy carbs. Get your daily allotment of carbs only from fruit, vegetables, legumes if allowed, nuts, seeds, dairy foods if allowed, and very limited amounts of whole grains. One carb is not just like another.

The best thing about low-carb eating is that when we do it the way we should, we eat loads of fresh, whole foods. Just because there are a ton of low-carb convenience foods available these days does not mean that you should be eating them. An occasional indulgence of sugar-free chocolate or reduced-carb fast food is OK, but relying on fake substitutes most of the time (or even daily) is a very, very bad idea.

Read the ingredient list and you'll see that most of these products are full of chemicals, preservatives, and other junk with very little real food added. Just because manufacturers are good at manipulating the ratios to display a low total carb count on the label doesn't mean it is good food; it just means it's edible—which is a long way from desirable.

Of course there are some exceptions. Some of the low-carb tortillas and cracker substitutes, for instance, are very good and contain mostly real food with very little added. Become a label reader! Choose your carbs wisely, always.

Bake your own sugar-free treats in preference to buying them. There are lots of good recipes available nowadays. (I have published two cookbooks myself.)

TIP: *Beware of artificial sweeteners known as polyols or sugar alcohols, which can affect people differently. Commonly reported side effects include gas and other intestinal upset, including diarrhea, elevated blood sugars and weight gain. Common sugar alcohols: maltitol, sorbitol, xylitol, erythritol, hydrogenated starch hydrolysates, isomalt, lactitol, and mannitol.*

Part 4

Suggestions for Shopping and Preparing Meals

Plan and prepare to succeed

Regular, advance food preparation is the single most important th[...]
dieters must do in order to succeed. It's really not difficult, even i[...]
know how to cook, except for being time-consuming. A lot like exercis[...]
that goes, but I assure you that both activities are worth your effort. I ca[...]
this enough—this can't be just another "diet." If you want to feel good, ha[...]
energy, have better health, and/or lose weight (and, most important, keep the[...]
weight off), then you will need to make lifelong, not just temporary, changes.

Fortunately, hunger is one thing you will not need to grow accustomed to when
living a low-carb lifestyle. It is imperative that you make good choices at all times,
however, and you will only do so when you have plenty of wholesome low-carb food
available. Most people will need to dedicate one day per week to food preparation.
If you work five days per week, spending an entire day in the kitchen can seem like
a burden, but it's worth it because it can make the rest of your week go so much
better. After a while it will become second nature to you to plan ahead, and you'll
find that you can spread the tasks out over the week, but while you are trying to
establish good low-carb eating habits, I recommend a regular, once-weekly shopping
and prep session.

Decide what you like to eat best from your allowable food list, and then shop accordingly. Go to your favorite grocery store or members' warehouse, and stock up.

Produce. Choose some green leafy veggies first from the produce section (romaine or leaf lettuce, endive, radicchio, escarole, spinach, kale, and so on). Next, select what you like from the following: asparagus, avocadoes, berries, broccoli, cauliflower, cantaloupe, celery, eggplant, daikon radish, hot and/or bell peppers, mushrooms, radishes, tomatoes, green beans, green onions and regular onions; and chayote, spaghetti, zucchini, or yellow crookneck squash. Avoid all root vegetables and fruits not previously mentioned, as well as any mentioned that might not fit into your particular eating plan.

Meat. Select meats you like to eat—good cuts of beef, ground beef, bacon and sausage, chicken, pork, and fish. If you want some more convenience-type meats, get some cans of tuna and chicken, deli meats (ask for nutritional info if it is not posted, since some deli meats are full of fillers and even sugars), or even hot dogs (Hebrew National and International Glatt brands don't add any sugar and are both kosher) or bratwurst. A favorite of mine for low-carb convenience is precooked bacon. It is packaged in layers and you can grab a few pieces anytime to heat in the microwave—though not as good as what you cook yourself, when speed is imperative, precooked can't be beat. Rotisserie chicken is usually acceptable, but it may be worth asking to see the ingredient list of any marinade they inject into the chicken before roasting it. Prepared buffalo wings are usually acceptable, too—just be sure to read every label, and don't be afraid to ask for nutritional information.

> *Stock up on the good stuff*

Oils. Get some good oils for cooking (unrefined macadamia and olive are the healthy oils that I use for cooking) and for things like salad dressings. Walnut and sesame oil are both great for salads but should never be heated.

Salad dressings. Get some salad dressings with no added sugar (check all labels), or, better yet, whip up some homemade dressings. Blue cheese, ranch, Caesar, and Italian are usually good choices, as are vinaigrettes. Other allowable condiments include real mayonnaise, seasoned vinegars, mustards without added sugars, hot sauces, and Worcestershire sauce (which has a trace of sugars, but the amount typically used does not present a problem for most people).

Nuts and fibers. If you can eat nuts, get some macadamias, almonds, pecans, hazelnuts, and/or walnuts—but pass up peanuts, pistachios, and cashews. Get some spicy pork rinds (trust me on this, they make a great substitute for bread crumbs in lots of recipes, even if you don't care to eat them as a snack). Wasa Fiber Rye Crispbread and La Tortilla Low Carb Tortillas are available in most grocery stores now and have a high fiber content, making them good choices.

Frozen foods. Be sure to go to the frozen-foods section and get some bagged legal veggies for busy nights when the fresh ones are just too much work. Buy canned black soybeans if you can find them. Canned vegetables such as tomatoes, green beans, and asparagus, are always good to have on hand in a pinch. Buy some frozen entrees like chicken tenders, pre-pressed burgers, and fish fillets—these can all go on the grill frozen and still be ready to eat in minutes!

Dairy products. If you can eat them, don't leave without a visit to the dairy section for some sour cream, cream cheese, cream, real butter, buttermilk if you like it, eggs, and cheese.

Prepare some food for later

If you get into a regular habit of prepping food, and even cooking some in advance, you'll be a lot less likely to blow your diet later in the week when time seems to be ticking away too rapidly. Here's the routine I've developed.

Salad greens. Most low-carb dieters will need plenty of clean salad greens. If you dislike the sour taste of prewashed salad greens, you will want to wash your own.

1. Fill a clean sink with a mixture of water and produce cleanser, and let the greens soak for a while.
2. Mix three heads of romaine or red leaf lettuce with one bunch of spinach and one small head of iceberg, for a nice mix of healthy, leafy, and crunchy.
3. Wash, peel, and chop other low-carb vegetables you like in your salads, and place them all in vacuum-seal containers. Well-dried lettuce can last for weeks without turning brown when vacuum-sealed. It will last up to a week when layered in clean toweling and then sealed in regular plastic bags, because the paper or cloth will absorb extra moisture.

Hard-boiled eggs. While my greens for the week are soaking, I hard-boil a dozen eggs. For easy peeling, use older eggs and prick a small hole in the wide end of each one with a pin or thumbtack. Always start them in cold water with a splash of vinegar and a spoonful of salt added. Once they come to a boil, turn off the heat, put on the lid, and allow them to sit in the hot water for 20 minutes. Pour off the hot water and replace it with ice water until the eggs are completely cool; then drain and refrigerate. The shells should slip right off when the time comes.

Chicken. Poaching chicken is best done at a very low simmer. Boiling toughens the meat proteins and causes that ugly scum to appear on top. I always save the liquid for use in soups or other meals, and either slice up the cooked meat for use in chef's salads or else chop it and add mayonnaise, along with lots of chopped celery and a little bit of red onion, salt, pepper, celery salt, and a teaspoon or so of lemon juice. Delicious chicken salad, ready at a moment's notice. Some weeks I make egg or tuna salad instead of, or in addition to, the chicken salad.

TIP: *Do not chop greens with a metal implement ahead of time, however, because that will cause the edges to turn brown prematurely.*

Breakfast. Plan breakfasts—make a batch of low-carb muffins or crustless mini quiche in muffin tins. Precook breakfast meats to save both time and mess. I like to bake both preformed sausage patties and bacon slices in the oven to save time and mess.

Casseroles. I make some sort of casserole each week and freeze it in individual portions, so that I can have a hot lunch anytime. Meatloaf is another good make-ahead meal—just replace the bread crumbs with low-carb ones or substitute Parmesan cheese, wheat bran, or textured vegetable protein.

Treats and sweets. Don't forget to attend to your sweet tooth and make some kind of artificially sweetened treat, unless you are one of the rare ones who can totally forgo that occasional pleasure. I am not; I would never have made it for the long haul without an occasional "sweet treat." And the long haul is what it is all about. Feeling deprived is what always led me to stop low-fat diets. I simply did not allow that to happen with low-carb—and neither should you! But do remember that most people lose more weight when indulging in homemade treats and staying away from packaged low-carb convenience foods, especially those with high concentrations of sugar alcohols such as maltitol (common in most premade sugar-free desserts).

Now, enjoy!

Now that you have stocked your low-carb kitchen, just think of all the great meals you can whip up.

Breakfast. For breakfast, you can choose from any sort of egg dish—hard-boiled eggs, omelets, crustless quiche, or my favorite—scrambled or fried eggs served with steak, ham, sausage or bacon, along with a thin wedge of cantaloupe. You can choose to eat cheese or any other meat, or even vegetables. Leftovers of all kinds make great breakfasts. Feel free to be creative. Here are some out-of-the-ordinary suggestions:

- A protein shake along with a handful of fresh berries and some nuts on the side
- A low-carb protein bar (although this should not become a habit by any means)
- Fiber crackers spread with cream cheese and low-carb fruit spread or smoked salmon
- Breakfast burritos, which are easy to fashion ahead of time out of taco meat or spicy sausage paired with things like onions, peppers, black soybeans, scrambled eggs, and cheese inside of a low-carb tortilla or homemade egg crepe. Wrap these individually and freeze, then wrap in a damp towel to reheat in the microwave.

Lunch. For lunch, choose from any protein source paired with a healthy vegetable. I usually try to have an entree salad such as steak sautéed with onions and peppers and cheese, served over a bed of greens in place of bread. Enjoy previously forbidden salad ingredients like real bacon, hard-boiled eggs, and chunks of blue cheese! Enjoy fancy salads with ingredients such as warm goat cheese and pecans. Other suggestions:

- Roll up sliced deli meats and cheese around celery sticks, pickles, or green onions
- Pile fiber crackers high with egg, chicken, or tuna salad
- Stuff egg, chicken, or tuna salad into celery sticks or hollowed-out tomatoes or peppers
- Wrap up sandwich fillings in a low-carb tortilla
- Use napa (Chinese) cabbage as a substitute for bread and make a sandwich. You can also use leaf lettuce, but sometimes if the leaf lettuce is thick and sturdy enough to hold sandwich ingredients together, it is a little bitter. Napa cabbage has a sturdy leaf and a mild flavor.

Snacks. For snacks, you can eat cream cheese in celery sticks, hard-boiled eggs, unsweetened yogurt, berries, sugar-free mousse or gelatin, melon, nuts, olives, cheese crisps, raw veggies with ranch dip, and pork rind or vegetable nachos with taco meat, refried black soybeans, salsa, guacamole, or sour cream.

Dinner. For dinner, the possibilities are truly endless. You can make a low-carb version of almost any meal you already like.

- Craving fried chicken? No problem: bread the chicken with egg and pork rinds, wheat bran, Parmesan cheese, or almond flour and then fry it as normal.
- Cream of mushroom or broccoli soup made with real butter and heavy cream is both heavenly and fast.
- Sauté chicken in butter and olive oil, pour in a little whipping cream and some Parmesan cheese, and you'll have delicious chicken alfredo with no effort. Eat it over steamed or stir-fried shredded cabbage or zucchini "noodles," broccoli, and cauliflower, or my favorite: fresh steamed green beans.
- Craving pizza? No problem: get some pepperoni; sauté some mushrooms, onions, and bell peppers; and combine them with some no-sugar-added tomato sauce and mozzarella cheese over the top of a cheese crisp or low-carb tortilla.
- Craving Mexican food? No problem: make fajitas with low-carb tortillas or tacos on cheese crisp shells, and you can enjoy real sour cream, guacamole, and cheese on top! Make red chili with black soybeans or green chili with pork or poultry.
- Enjoy filet mignon or grilled salmon and steamed asparagus, broccoli. or cauliflower with cheese or Hollandaise sauce over the top.
- Enjoy stir-fry (without the starch) of beef and broccoli.
- Enjoy grilled chicken topped with bacon, melted cheese, and mushrooms.

The key word here is *enjoy*. If you'll just concentrate on all the wonderful food combinations you can eat, you will find yourself thinking less and less about those few things you are no longer choosing to eat. Low-carb eating is far more versatile than low-fat eating, but it does require a change in mind-set. Become a label reader! When I started eating this way, I literally spent hours in the grocery store going down the aisles and reading labels. I found some surprises and learned a lot. Eating low-carb is easy, and it should never be repetitive or boring—not when your menu choices are so varied and abundant.

Part 5

Additional Resources

Recommended reading

- *Cooking TLC: Truly Low Carb Cooking Volume I*, by Karen Rysavy (Truly Low Carb, Inc.; ISBN: 0971492913)
- *More Cooking TLC: Truly Low Carb Cooking Volume II*, by Karen Rysavy (Truly Low Carb, Inc.; ISBN: 0971492921)
- *LowCarb Energy* magazine (Coincide Media, L.L.C.; www.lowcarbenergy.com)
- *The Secrets of Low-Carb Success*, by Laura Richard, B.S.N., M.S.A (Kensington Publishing Corp.; ISBN: 0758206232)
- *Play Your Carbs Right!...With the Brennans*, by Theodore M. Brennan, Ellen C. Brennan (Wimmer Cookbooks; ISBN: 0966351932)
- *Eat Yourself Thin Like I Did*, by Nancy Moshier, R.N. (Nancy's Cookbooks; ISBN: 0970102909)
- *Eat Yourself Thin With Fabulous Desserts*, by Nancy Moshier, R.N. (Nancy's Cookbooks; ISBN: 0970102917)
- *Living Low-Carb: The Complete Guide to Long Term Low-Carb Dieting*, by Fran McCullough (Little, Brown; ISBN: 0316089761)
- *Nutrition & Physical Degeneration*, by Weston A. Price (McGraw-Hill; ISBN: 0879838167)
- *LowCarb Living* magazine (CappMedia, Inc.; www.lowcarblivingmag.com)
- *Living the Low Carb Life from Atkins to the Zone*, by Jonny Bowden, M.A., C.N.S. (Sterling; ISBN: 1402713983)

Online resources

Official Diet Sites
Atkins site: www.atkins.com
Beyond Atkins site: www.totalhealthdoc.com
Carbohydrate Addict's Diet site: www.carbohydrateaddictsdiet.com
GO-Diet site: www.go-diet.com
Hamptons Diet site: www.hamptonsdiet.com
Neanderthin site: www.sofdesign.com/neander
Protein Power Site: www.eatprotein.com
South Beach site: www.southbeachdiet.com
Sugar Busters! site: www.sugarbusters.com
The Zone site: www.zonediet.com

Other Web Sites
Active Low-Carber Forums: www.lowcarber.org
Carb Awareness Council: www.carbaware.org
CarbHealth: www.carbhealth.com
CarbWire: www.carbwire.com
FitDay: www.fitday.com
Karen Rysavy: www.trulylowcarb.com and www.learnlowcarb.com
Low Carb Cafe: www.lowcarbcafe.com
Low Carb Consumers League: www.lowcarbconsumersleague.com
Low Carb Eating: www.lowcarbeating.com
Low Carb Exercise: www.lowcarbexercise.com
Low Carb Luxury: www.lowcarbluxury.com
Lowcarbiz: www.lowcarbiz.com
Nutrition Data: www.nutritiondata.com
USDA site: www.nal.usda.gov/fnic/cgi-bin/nut_search.pl
Weston A. Price Foundation: www.westonaprice.org

Index

appetite, 11
Atkins, Robert C., 5, 14

Banting, William, 4
blood sugar, 17
breakfasts, 52, 53

calories, 32
carbohydrates
  counting, 39
  defined, 7
  hidden, 39, 40
casseroles, 52
cholesterol, 23, 34, 41

dairy products, 50
depression, 43
diet plans, 13–28
  Atkins Nutritional
Approach, 14
  Beyond Atkins, 27
  Carbohydrate Addict's
    Diet, 21
  choosing, 13
  GO-Diet, 22
  Hamptons Diet, 28
  Insulin Resistance
    Diet, 25
  Life Without Bread, 23
  Neaderthin, 18
  Protein Power, 5, 15
  Schwarzbein
    Principle, 20

Somersizing, 19
South Beach Diet, 26
Sugar Busters!, 17
Your Fat Can Make You
  Thin, 24
Zone, The, 16
dietary supplements, 38
dinners, 54

Eades, Drs. Michael and
  Mary Dan, 5, 15, 38
education
  on cholesterol levels, 34
  staying informed, 41
EFAs (essential fatty
  acids), 38
exercise, 37

family pressure, 43
fats
  defined, 7
  diet plans and, 20, 24, 25
  "good" and "bad," 15
  low-carb diets and, 11
  weight loss and, 32
fibers, 50
food combining, 19
food diaries, 39
frozen foods, 50

glucose, 7, 8
glycemic index, 17

hard-boiled eggs, 51
hidden carbohydrates, 39, 40

insulin, 8, 9, 25
insulin resistance, 6, 21, 25

junk foods, 46

ketoacidosis, 30
ketones, 27, 30, 31, 36
ketosis, 10, 12, 27, 30
kidneys, 10, 25, 27, 30

low-carb diets. See also diet
  plans; meals; myths
  appetite when starting, 11
  benefits of, 9
  choosing, 2
  deemphasizing scale
weight, 45
  defined, 3
  dietary supplements
    and, 38
  effects of, 10–12
  exercise and, 37
  food diaries and carb
    counting for, 39–40
  history of, 4–5
  junk foods, 46
  long-term health risks, 33
  resisting family pressure, 43
  staying informed, 41
  sugar, 44

support groups for, 42
types of, 13–28
water consumption, 36
why they work, 6–9
lunches, 53

meals, 48–54
  breakfasts, 52, 53
  dinners, 54
  food selection, 11
  lunches, 53
  preparing food ahead,
      48, 51–52
  shopping, 49
  snacks, 54
  treats, 46, 52
  variety in, 53–56
meat, 49, 51
myths
  cholesterol levels, 34
  dangers of ketosis, 30

fewer calories as, 32
ketone measurement
    required, 31
long-term health
    risks, 33

nuts, 25, 26, 50

oils, 25, 28, 38, 50, 59
online resources, 57

potassium, 10, 38
Price, Weston A., 4
processed foods, 28, 44, 46
produce, 49

recommended reading, 56
Rysavy, Karen, 60

salads and dressings, 50–51
shopping, 48

snacks, 54
Stefansson, 4
sugar, 7, 44
sugar alcohols, 39, 46
support groups, 42

treats, 46, 52
triglycerides, 34

uric acid, 25

vegetarians, 6

water consumption, 36
weight
  deemphasizing scale, 45
  exercise, 37
  fats role in loss of, 32
  food diaries and carb
      counting, 39–40

Karen Rysavy started a low-carb diet more than four years ago, after her husband announced his intention to do so. Initially concerned about his safety, she did research that ultimately made a believer out of her. One year later, she was ten sizes and 65 pounds lighter, and her husband lost an equal amount in even less time. Both made improvements in their health, with Karen lowering her blood cholesterol by hundreds of points after just the first two months.

"I had tried low-fat diets and even medication designed to lower cholesterol, but my cholesterol and my weight both continued to go up," she said. "Low-carb is the first and only thing that helped me. Now that I live a low-carb lifestyle, I am never hungry, I enjoy all my food, and, believe it or not, I am eating lots more fruits and especially vegetables than ever before. I never have energy slumps these days. Before I changed my eating habits, I never had any energy, period. Now I never stop moving—or smiling! This is not a diet for me—diet implies something temporary—for me this is a lifestyle, and it is one that I love!"

Karen self-published two low-carb cookbooks before writing *Learn the Low-Carb Lifestyle* for Fair Shake Press. She has a popular low-carb support Web site (www.trulylowcarb.com), and is an associate editor for *LowCarb Energy* magazine. The late Robert Atkins, M.D., recognized her in October 2001 by publishing her success story on the Atkins Center Web site, and he later quoted her in his last diet book, *Atkins for Life*.